POGO:
WE HAVE MET THE ENEMY AND HE IS US

Walt Kelly

SIMON AND SCHUSTER, NEW YORK

10   11   12   13   14   15

This is for
    SELBY,
        who slogged
            on foot the
                entire
                    distance.

CONTENTS

WHERE THE WASTIES REPOSE

Where will the
   wandering wasties
     repose?

In a clump. In a lump.
On Grandaddle's nose.

Gramps Ebenezer,
a teasering,
speasering,
wheezering
Sneezer.

A spreadening,
   deadening,
   dipsy Diseaser.

Ungamely, bad-aimly, not-blamely
    old Geezer
And all becausely the Fauseleys repose
     on the length
     in the breadth
     of Grampolly's nose.

THE MANY FACETED PUBLIC EYE

The eye of the public, like that of the insect, has many facets, and these enable each creature to look fore, aft, overhead and sideways. There the similarity ends, for the insect has at least six legs and sometimes a double set of wings. This equipment enables him to alertly spring toward his prey, away from his enemy or in pursuit of his mate. Humans, on the other hand, are generally two-legged, fumble-fingered slobs whose indolent wits enable them by and large to be sitting ducks.

We have seen what we have done before, creating such mounds of rubbage that whole civilizations have been forced to move, usually northward to avoid the flies. Slowly and painstakingly we have discovered that garbage causes disease, that was with the rear view facets. Sideways we have seen a place to dump. Straight ahead we have seen the clear and clean promise of tomorrow, forgetting that, so far as the goal goes, we are on the starting tape exactly even with the slop we have just flung over our shoulder.

Naturally, if something oppressive looms in the neighborhood, we look for someone to blame it on. The need for a scapegoat has been the foundation of entire religious movements. So with the facets of our eyes blinking like fireflies we look about and zero in on *somebody*.

The Somebody we fasten upon is hardly ever the lady next door whose cellar is awash with broken jam jars and mice. It's never our son whose bedroom might dismay Hercules. It's not us, to be sure, whose trash cans are broken, whose attic deserves a citation from the fire department. No, we pick on somebody identifiable and big. Somebody with smokestacks, with thundering waste pipes dumping glop into the river or lake or ocean. And rightly so. WE don't go that big, now do we?

The big polluter did not start out with smokestacks. He didn't start pumping gunk into the waters of our world when he was six years old. He started small. Throwing papers underfoot in the streets, heaving old bottles into vacant lots, leaving the remnants of a picnic in the fields and woodlands. Just like the rest of us.

At last the stuff is catching up to us. Man has turned out to be his own worst enemy. If the many faceted eye of the Public had at least one facet inwardly directed which would tell Man something of himself, the view might be so clear that we would finally see tomorrow.

What follows is a view of what currently makes up an educational film explanation of just who is responsible for pollution.

W.K.

14

15

16

17

CALL OUT THE **DRAGNET!** US POLICE UNDERSTAND A CATASTROPHE IS IN PROGRESS.

19

A GUN AIN'T LOADED 'TIL YOU PULL THE TRIGGER

IT'S GOTTA STOP!

SOME *CULPRIT* TRIED TO DROWND A *CHILD DOG!*

AN INNOCENT TAD ON THE THRESHOLD OF *DESIRABLE* DOGDOM...

... AND SOME *FIEND* BEFOULING THE SWIMMING HOLE WITH EXPENDABLE *JUNK* TRIED TO SABOTAGE THE INFANT'S CAREER... AN *INSULT* TO ALL *DOGS!*

22

OF COURSE NOT! *WHAT'S MORE DANGEROUS THAN A LOADED GUN?*

BAM!

WHAT'S MORE DANGEROUS THAN A *LOADED* GUN?

A *UNLOADED* GUN?

FROM HERE ON UP, IT'S ALL DOWNHILL

BY JING! YOU TADS GO GIT WASHED.... I'M 'BOUT TO POUR THE FRESH WATER INTO THE RICE TO GET THE **PERLOO** READY FOR SUPPER!

WHOO BOY! SOUNDS **DEE**-LICIOUS!

CAN'T WAIT!

WHAT IN THE WORLD IS PERLOO?

YOU **GOT** ME.

I BE NABBED! *CRANFORD CRAWFISH!*

WHAT YOU DOIN' THERE, CRANFORD? YOU AIN'T ON THE MENU.

ALBERT, ALL'S I COME ABOARD FOR WAS SO'S I COULD GET TO **BREATHE**.

ME AN' MY PAL WAS SETTIN' ON THE **BOTTOM** TRYIN' TO GET A BREATH OF **FRESH AIR**, WHEN YOUR BUCKET COME BY.

26

"LET'S HITCH A *RIDE!*" SAYS MY PAL, "LET'S GET ALOFT AN' BREATHE *FRESH AIR!*"

HE SAYS, "WE'LL START LIFE ANEW ··· AN' STOP BREATHIN' OL' *BICYCLE SPROCKETS!*"

'CAUSE *NOW* LOOK AT HIM!

ONE OF NATURE'S NOBLEMEN ··· WITH A *CLO'ESPIN* ON HIS *SNOZ!*

WITHOUT IT HE *CAN'T* BREATHE.

HOW DO HE BREATHE *WITH* IT?

DON'T BOTHER ME WITH DETAILS! JUST TAKE A WHIFF OF *THAT* UP THERE!

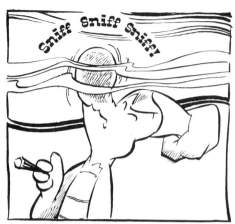

Sniff Sniff Sniff!

SEE... IT DON'T PAY TO INHALE *STRAIGHT AIR.*

GACK!

SOMEDAY THE **SURGEON GENERAL** GONNA DISCOVER THAT **BREATHIN'** IS **HARMFUL** TO YOUR HEALTH.

SO ME AN' MY PAL GONNA HEAD FOR THE **OPEN ATLANTIC OCEAN.**

HEY, ALBERT, IS THAT *YOU* MAKIN' THAT **3-ALARM** *STENCH?*

NO! IT COMIN' OFF THE **FORT MUDGE MEMORIAL DUMP!**

31

JUST BECAUSE **I'M** A **PIG**...

BAM!

YOU **IS A PIG!** CAUSIN' SUCH A **LOUD** STENCH A MAN NEEDS **EARPLUGS!** MAKIN', LIKE I SAY, A **DUMP** OUT OF OUR **DUMP!**

WHO **ME?** A **HONEST MAN** EKIN' OUT A LIVIN' FOR HIS CHILDREN?

AN' WHO'S TEACHIN' THE DEAR TADS A **TRADE** AT THE **SAME** TIME?

WHERE'S ALL THIS STUFF *COME FROM!?*

BEFORE US REG'LAR PIGS CAN MESS AROUND WITH THIS STUFF, *SOME OTHER PIG* GOTTA *THROW IT AWAY!*

SUCH AS THIS *TASTY OL' TOWEL HERE* ...

WHICH I WAS *ENJOYIN'* BEFORE I WAS SO RUDELY *INTERRUPTED.*

ORG! MINE!

POGO

IT'S ALL *YOUR FAULT,* POGO!

WE'RE BETRAYED BY OUR FRIENDS! WHILST ALL US *GOOD FOLKS* IS LEADIN' *BLAMELESS LIVES*...

OTHERS, CARELESS, *UNMINDFUL* OF THEIR *NEIGHBORS,* DUMPS AS THEY PLEASES...

DESTROYIN' THE COUNTRY FOR US ... *HUH?*

ALBERT

AN' THESE OL' *RAZZLE BAGS* AN' *FRIMMY FRAMS* AN' *GOOGLE LOBS* ALL BELONG---

ALBERT

38

THE LEGAL LEAGUE ILLEGAL EAGLE

THE LAW ASSUMES EVERY MAN IS INNOCENT...

UNTIL ...

... CAUGHT.

42

PITY THE POOR RAT

I live a
very humble
life,

Crowded by my own,

Complaining
not of bug
nor mice,

Seldomly I moan.

In sewer pipes
    where willy nils
And poly glots the gloom
I cuddle in my cribbish chills
To ruminate my room ---

And if I venture forth
    to please
My mate with chancey cheese
And return from dungeon danger
With a piece of yet a stranger ---

Why view me with
    open anger,
Am I then a
    doppelganger?

Within the wall I'm
    merry, mild;
And, given all, your
    very child.

44

ROACHES ARE READ; VILEST BREW ~~

A cockroach I, might
I intrude,
Or encroach by night
all in nude?

Window shopping.
Table hopping.
Interloping.
Misanthroping.

If nothing's slopped
to make me stay
Allow me to recite

I'm a real, real gone
bug by day
And a drop-out ~~~
fly-by-night.

H₂O IS H. TO PAY

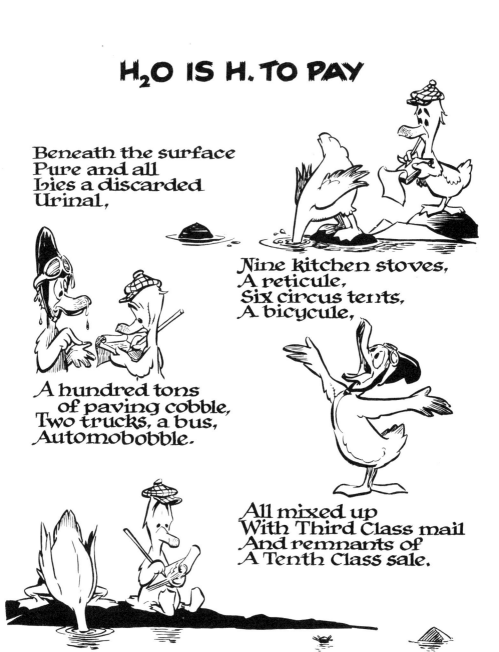

Beneath the surface
Pure and all
Lies a discarded
Urinal,

Nine kitchen stoves,
A reticule,
Six circus tents,
A bicycule,

A hundred tons
of paving cobble,
Two trucks, a bus,
Automobobble.

All mixed up
With Third Class mail
And remnants of
A Tenth Class sale.

Left-overs from
a disrupt home,
The daily garbage,
bugs of loam.

Here is water you
cannot drink;
Swim in it and
you've got to sink.

Slow,
The thought
Gets through
Your bonnet:

Don't drink!
Don't swim!
Walk
Upon it.

WE ARE COMING IN A HEAD BEHIND

Between the halves here, looking ahead, we look backward to the year that's gone before. The ensuing collection of small work features Wily Catt and Seminole Sam attempting to abduct the Pup-dog because they have on good authority (their own) that he is worth a million dollars. We have a new group in the swamp causing new cleavages between twig and limb. Problems abound, gossip is rampant. Between the bad ear and the bad mouth lies an idle brain. None of the problems are solved, a blessing, for a problem solved is no longer a problem and what would our children have left to do?

The other day a newspaper reported that the questions asked by Ed Murrow twenty years ago go unanswered. A West German member of parliament declares that despite a lot of talking, Americans are largely inarticulate. We have boasted that given a place to stand, we can move the world. Well, where do we stand? It's time to move.

A SECRET SHARED IS A SECRET BARED.

A WISE MAN KNOWS HIS OWN BURGLAR.

BE PREPARED ...
... AND HIDE.

SEEK,
SEEKER,
SEEKRET.

A NAP
OF KIDNAPPERS.

68

69

CONDUCTING
THE INDUCEMENT
OF DEDUCTION.

ANOTHER
RING ON THE
BOOMERANG.

9-7

76

9-15

THE PLURAL
OF MAN
IS WOMAN.

80

THE RIGHT EYE
NEVER KNOWS WHAT
THE WRONG EYE KNOWS.

BLOWING THAT **COMPUTER** UP IN MY FACE EVERY TIME I VISIT....*HRAMPH!*

UM.... *WHAT'S THIS?*

WE'RE **GYPSIES**, MOLE....WORKIN' OUT A PRICE ON OUR **MILLION DOLLAR PUP DOG.**

9-17

STOLEN, NO DOUBT. WHAT YOU BIRDS NEED IS A **FENCE**.

AROUND **WHAT?**

NO, HE MEANS A GUY TO GET RID OF THE DOG FOR A **PRICE**--- THEN HE TAKES FIFTY PERCENT.... I CALL IT *ROBBERY*.

WELL.... FIFTY PERCENT OF **SOMETHING** IS BETTER THAN 50% OF *NOTHING*.

WHAT'S ALL THIS ABOUT US NEEDIN' A **FENCE** FOR THE PUP DOG?

Y'SEE, THE PUP DOG HERE IS A **HOT PROPERTY**... SO YOU NEED A DEALER TO **UNLOAD** IT.... SELL IT FOR YOU.

9-21

AND THAT DEALER RETAINS A **MODEST FEE** FOR HIS SERVICES--- SAY FIFTY PERCENT.

83

THERE'S NOTHING
LIKE A LITTLE
HONESTY.

10-6

THE SECOND BELT
COMES BEFORE
THE FIRST.

90

CONSTITUTIONAL CONSTITUENTS.

93

This completely secret message evidently applies to adults ···

AYE

10-27

We are concerned with children, however.

SO WE JUST CUT THE MESSAGE DOWN TO SIZE··· SNIP A BIT FROM EITHER END ··· HEAD OR FEET···

Heads: they can't think··· Feet: they can't run.

A GREAT SUGGESTION ···SNIP FROM BOTH ENDS.

KILL THE EMPIRE!

NOTHING LIKE
COLD WATER
IF IT'S BEER.

I'LL PUT THESE DISHES IN THE TUB HERE AND SEE IF HE GETS THE **IDEA.**

YES, IT CERTAINLY IS A **PLEASURE** TAKIN' CARE OF A LITTLE DOG. A **SMART** ONE.

HEY, MOLE! DIDN'T YOU GET US THAT **FENCE** YET?!

EGAD, SEMINOLE SAM! MY OLD FRIEND, THE **FOX!** HOW GOOD TO SEE YOU!

10-21

NEVER MIND THE **GUFF!**

SAY ... WHAT YOU GOT THAT LITTLE OL' PUP DOG **DOIN'?** SWEEPIN'!?

DOGGONE! YOU CAN'T WORK A CHILD LIKE THAT, MOLE ...

YOU GOTTA GET THE SPRAT A **SMALLER** BROOM.

101

A BAD EAR
IS WORSE THAN
A BAD MOUTH.

104

NOT S'POSED TO TELL···· BUT THEY SAY THE **COMPUTER** IS A *DRINKER*··· ····**WILD HORSES** COULDN'T DRAG IT OUTTA ME BUT YOU'RE A LI'L *DIFF'RENT.*

BUT, M'SIEUR **POGO**, THESE ARE THE TALK IN EVERY **ALL** THOSE **BOUTIQUE** IN LE FORT MUDGE.

BOY····GLAD TO HEAR *THAT*··· I WOULDN'T WANNA BE BREAKIN' ANY **CONFIDENCES.**

YEP···YOU'D BE SURPRISED··· OL' **MOLE** GOT THE **SKUNK CHILD** OVER'T HIS PLACE····· MOLE THINKS IT'S THE *PUP DOG*··HAW! AN' WHAT'S MORE HE'S WAITIN' ON HIM HAND AN' FOOT.

11-1

11-5

108

WHO'S THE RESIDENT PRESIDENT?

110

ONLY BITE WITH YOUR OWN TEETH.

THAT POST CARD FROM MR. OSSINING WHO WANTS TO BUY DYNAMITE **ON TIME**, 'CAUSE THAT'S WHAT HE'S DOIN' ANYWAY, REMINDS ME OF A **TEEVY** FELLER I KNEW....

MIGGLE'S MARKET LTD.
BY APPOINTMENT TO HER MAJESTY

11-17

HE WANTED TO SELL TIME TO **LEAVENWORTH**

BUT THEY HAD A DAGBLAG *PLENTY*, HUH?

FIGGERS

AYUP

POGO'S NEW PAPER SAYS "'PUP DOG' KIDNAPPED"

GORK!

FORT MUDGE MOST

11-18

"SUCH WAS THE FIRST ALARM YESTERDAY. CONCERN FOR THE SMALL DOG WAS RAMPANT....

116

C'MON... NOW'S OUR **CHANCE**... WE'LL STEP BRAVELY FORWARD, GRAB HIM BY THE LAPELS AN'...

HE GOT ON A SWEATER.

OKAY... AFTER *YOU*, GENTS.

I'LL LOOK INTO THE **GARBAGE PAIL**... SEE WHAT THEY HAD FOR SUPPER.

A VALUABLE SOCIAL ITEM.

GOOD THING I DISGUISED MYSELF WITH THIS SPANISH MOSS... **DEACON'S** ON THE BACK PORCH.

12-8

Me, a administrative advisor, put to work peeling knockwursts and other vegetables.

~~~sigh~~~

Gadzooks! The wurst fights back.

Chomp!

BETTER
WURST
'TIL THE END.

WE COME TO FIND OUT WHO'S *DEE*-NOUNCIN' THE **PREXY.**

LET ME CONSULT MY LIST OF WHAT I'VE DENOUNCED RECENTLY: **TEEVY, RADIO, NEWSPAPERS, BOOKS, BRAINS, RELIEF,** THE **EAST,** THE **NORTH, COLLEGE KIDS, NON-**COLLEGE KIDS, *UM*···· NO, **NOT** THE **CHIEF**···· NOT EVEN UNDER **MISC.**

12-15

FEEL FREE TO LOOK AROUND···· YOU DON'T SEEM BRIGHT ENOUGH TO CAUSE HARM.

THIS PLACE IS KINDA **SCAREY**···AND US WITHOUT NO **PROTECTION.**

I GOT A WEAPON···· I STOLE A SALAMI.

124